IN SEARCH OF THE COLOR
Yellow

K.L. Schoberg

Orange Hat Publishing
www.orangehatpublishing.com - Waukesha, WI

For information, please contact:

Orange Hat Publishing
www.orangehatpublishing.com
Waukesha, WI

Photography by Anthony Larson
Cover typography by Kelly Maddern

Orange Hat
PUBLISHING

www.orangehatpublishing.com

for those who believed the sky was blue
but searched to find the golden hues

VOLUME 1

VOLUME 2

VOLUME 1

A DISTANT BELL

Barefoot I trotted
A wooded path
To an open wheat field
Many times, I had passed

Goldenrod swished
And swayed with ease
Whispering my secrets
To the summer breeze

Amidst the piles
Of fallen birch
Sat a decaying
Vacant church

Over the threshold
Through open door
Stood an altar where children
Prayed, no more

Though I trespassed
This sacred space,
I uttered aloud,
"Is this my place?"

Through brokenness, I stepped
A crackling path
To a sun-danced window
Of shattered glass

In silent reverence,
Hollowed, yet whole
I held onto hope,
As a distant bell tolled

WHERE DOES THE TUMBLEWEED ROLL?

Where does the tumbleweed roll?

Does it follow the song
Of a long-lost crow?
Does it amble through alleys
Venture the valleys
Wander and dither
Or float with the river?

Where does the tumbleweed roll?
I followed it once
On a sun-kissed day
It rolled through a field
It rolled where it may
It rolled over a hill
Then it rolled away

Where does the tumbleweed roll?

Some things in life we cannot see
Just let it roll, just let it free
Someday when the west wind blows
I have faith it will roll back to me

STUBBORN HEART AND A CLOUD

I will never see the same cloud twice
Though I stare at the sky and try

I wait and wait, a perished fate
No particular reason why

Smoke billows by
Egrets fly
Even cranes
Concede and comply

A sparrow
An arrow
Fly low
Stretch high

I wait through snow
I wait through rain
I wait through hail
I wait through pain

Though my point is quite concise
I will never see the same cloud twice

THE WOMAN ON TOP OF THE HILL

How many times have I had this dream
Of a swaying field of wheat?
Sunrays upon my wakening face,
A sweet aroma in the wind, just a trace.

Though my path was a hazy start,
I knew the way to go by heart.
On the outskirts of a forest lush,
I climbed the hillside through the brush.

Melting with every gentle step,
My cares of the real world simply left.
I took the path along the wood
To the top where a mansion stood.

On the front porch swayed a wooden swing,
An old woman waited to hear a story sing.
Though she wasn't anyone I knew,
Sitting next to her felt right to do.

When I spoke, the world was hushed,
As if my words should not be rushed.
She listened as minutes simply froze
Not once confused by words I chose.

What a strange thing to only breathe
Summer air inside my lucid dream.
As if she exists to wait for me
With the kindest eyes I've never seen.

Some nights I lay my head to sleep,
I think of her, and secrets we keep.
Then I awake in a field of wheat,
I follow the trail, and the dream repeats.

SECRETS OF THE EGRETS

What secrets do the egrets keep
As they swish and swoon and softly sweep?
What do they wish when they're sound asleep?
What secrets do the egrets keep?

What happens to swans before the dawn?
What do they rest their hopes upon?
What will they dream when clouds are gone?
What happens to swans before the dawn?

What are the rumors of the old black crow
As he muddles and fuddles to and fro?
What are the candid cries no one knows?
What are the rumors of the old black crow?

Perhaps we will never truly know
The stories of egrets, swans, and crows.
Yes, I understand. It's completely fine.
But I would tell them every secret of mine.

THE KEEPER OF THE LIGHTHOUSE

Wind-drunk waves tumble and spill
Driftwood crashes, seagulls shrill

The ocean's full of unmarked graves
Of seamen lost to violent waves

Lightning flares the charcoal sky
The captain begs the question why

Moonlit vessel thrashed at sea
No soul can hear his fading plea

He grasps the craft's trembling wheel
Final voyage, fate is sealed

Rhythmic spark, he eyes a light
A tower guards the captain's plight

Through the watchman's hole of glass
She waits for sinking ships to pass

But the warden of the radiant light
Is the one in need of rescue at night

Countless times, she climbs the tower
Summer squalls, the midnight hour

The captain eyes her empty gaze
Through the mist and thundery haze

He steers his sinking ship ashore
Easing burden freely born

He climbs the winding tower stairs
The moon ignites her auburn hair

She turns to see the captain's face
Collapsing into his embrace

I LEFT OUR WAS TO FIND MY IS

I mountain my pain and bag the rain
I up our rights and down our wrongs

I mourn our then but walk my now
Though I sometimes fight the which and how

Perhaps I cry for why and then
and wish for again, and again, and again

THE TOURISTS

Meet me in a cliffside village in Greece
Nibbling on olives, bread, and feta cheese
Let us drink red wine from a king-sized chalice
Let us tour as lost lovers through a Grecian Palace
Let us smell the markets and saline wind gust
Kiss me in the village, for only you I trust.

Meet me on a park bench in Tokyo, Japan
Holding butterfly parasols of yellow and tan
Let us drink from golden teacups, a sweet berry wine
Let us wander through shrines and temples divine
Let us smell blossoms from a budding tree in spring
Kiss me on the park bench where I gave an engagement ring.

Meet me in a castle in England
Nestled in the woods, seven towers stand
Let us drink from goblets, a royal champagne
Let us explore mysteries the fortress walls contain
Let us dance freely to the orchestra at the ball
Kiss me on our honeymoon, upon the stone wall.

Meet me in Boothbay Harbor, off the Gulf of Maine
Sitting on a fishing pier, clouds of lurking rain
Let us eat lobster and drink amber bottles of beer
Let us watch diving seagulls ascend then draw near
Let us search whipping waters for whales
Kiss me on the pier, for you I trail.

Meet me in a hospital, in a gown I shall lay
Gently hold me, my eyes are too tired to cry
Let us grasp an empty glass, I no longer drink
Let us hear the monitor, our hearts beat out of sync
Let us share our life stories and gently retell
Kiss me in a hospital, hold me close, and say farewell.

GIRL AT THE BUS STOP

She waits at the bus stop
Every morning at 7:52 a.m.
Bobbing to an unknown tune on her headphones
Warming the chill of the November wind.

Parked at a stoplight in my Honda Pilot
Paused in heavy traffic
I change the station from the
Annoying salesman's rant,

"No credit, low credit, no problem!"
I watch the girl at the bus stop and wonder
Where is she going?
Where did she buy her yellow bomber jacket
With the fake furry hood?

I think to myself,
I should write a poem about her.
The light turns green
I turn too sharply onto George Street
Missing the semi in oncoming traffic
Lost in my curious state of mind.

I park the car, three minutes early at 7:57 a.m.
And wonder, maybe she is in the back of the bus
Diverting eye contact from the red-bearded man
Who boarded after her.

Her tennis shoe crunches
Upon a Snickers wrapper.

***

I wait at the bus stop
Every morning at 7:52 a.m.
Listening to classical music on my headphones,
I feel the November wind on my neck.

Parked at a stoplight in her Honda Pilot
Paused in heavy traffic
I wonder why she stares at me,
Her eyes diverted to the radio dials.

I know she's looking at me,
Wondering, judging, guessing where I'm going
As I shiver in my yellow bomber jacket
Purchased at JCPenney after my shift as a cashier.

I think to myself,
"Watch where you're going, jerk,
You almost ran into that semi."

DREAM SONNET

Some nights I dream of spinning whirls of dust
Of running from a breach of inner trust

What brings the fear of wind into the night?
'Tis just another lover's sudden flight

Some nights I dream of falling off a cliff
A momentary bliss with hope, I drift

What brings the fear of sinking to abyss?
'Tis just another plunging wish amiss

Some nights I dream I lose you on a beach
I search in vain, but you I cannot reach

What brings the sudden fear of loss and fret?
'Tis just an aching breath of my regret

Some nights I dream of spinning whirls of dust
Of running from a breach of inner trust

ODE TO PECULIAR PEOPLE

Three cheers for the curious ones,
The poets who lay awake
Writing awkward puns.
The artists, the dreamers,
The legend believers,
The ones who trawl alone,
And the treasure seekers.

I once met an unusual man,
He sat upon a curb
Playing air accordion.
He tapped a happy tune,
A swaying Swedish waltz
As people danced by
Staring at his faults.

I once met a peculiar girl
Tattered hair in locks.
She jumped rope to a rap
From a battered boombox.
She hummed a joyful song,
But people laughed and jeered.
I have no idea why
They thought this girl was weird.

I once met an old woman
Who sat alone in pain.
She whistled at a bus stop
Waiting for a train.
The neighbors often talked
They said she was insane!
Though some day we all
May do the very same.

CHICKEN FROM A VAN IN HANALEI

Oceanview pier
'long Pacific shore,
Can I stay just
One day more?
Help me find
A way to pay!
I'll wash double rainbows
Off Moloa's Bay.

Waterfall town
Down graveled road,
Glistening waters
Ebbed and flowed.
I beg the question,
How can I stay?
I'll sell leis on the sands
Of old Pompei.

Mountainside village
Through the valley way,
I wish, I wish
To return one day.
I plea the query,
How can I stay?
I'll sell chicken
From a van in Hanalei.

THE LONGING

Near the space
Where secrets sleep
I dreamed a dream
I couldn't keep

I masked desire
I buried it deep
Near the abyss
Cold wind creeps

Last night I awoke
On a midnight street
A hungry heart
Amidst defeat

From darkness rose
A stranger's face
Two arms offered
Covert embrace

Moments slipped
Before the dawn
He gently kissed me
Then, was gone

Near the crevice
Where secrets sleep
Lays every dream
I couldn't keep

FISHERMAN'S HAIKU

White silence ripples
Solitary boat at dawn
Cast through fog, repeat

GREGORY BORDAN

The first time I saw him,
He was exiting a plane.
Our carry-on bags collided
As we walked through the tunnel.

He glanced at his wristwatch,
As he glided down the escalator
Two breaths in front of me.
Baggage tag said, "Gregory Bordan."

He politely smiled as I asked him
To know me with my eyes.
Quickly, he ghosted through
Glass doors and grabbed a taxi.

Years later, I lingered in line
At a coffee house. The barista
Said the name on his credit card,
"Gregory Bordan."

He ordered a caramel latte,
A cranberry scone, and hope.
Then he sat next to the window,
God rays showering his laptop.

"I remember you." I hovered,
Sipping my tea and desire.
"You were on my flight from Boston,
Two seats in front of me."

"Gregory Bordan." He shook my hand.
"I remember you too." He politely smiled,
Asking to know me with his eyes.
We shared words for hours.

The next time I saw him
We were lovers, walking together,
A plain gold band on our hands
Asking to know each other, again and again.

CHINESE BRUSH PAINTER

A Chinese brush painter
Does not paint a tree,
Rather, she captures
The essence of a tree

This is how I
Remember you

Tinted fragments of time,
Faded strokes of memory

I recollect the nature
Of you. Your kindness,
Your warmth, your soft hands

I think of you in vibrant hues,
Fallen leaves from
A bamboo tree,
Juniper green

The spirit of who we were
On the silk paper of recollection
Called Remorse

THE MEDICINE MAN

With potions of plenty and herbs in a can,
He's a healer, a dealer, a medicine man.

I'm allergic to chickens, rabbits, and goats,
My TV, my cell phone, my favorite coat,
My bed sheets, my couch, and my dog Pete.
Oh, how I wish this list was complete!

I can't have chocolate, wine, or caffeine,
I can't knit scarves with Aunt Irene.
I sneeze at my pillows, I cough at the willows,
When I walk barefoot, my belly billows.

No, these things I cannot fake.
I can't even gorge a birthday cake!
I'm allergic to wheat, gluten, and rye.
I get lumps in my throat and eagle eyes.

I'm allergic to cotton and polyester,
My sister Pam, and my best friend Lester.
While all this makes me run and holler,
I've already paid five hundred dollars!

He'll heal my woes and find my cure.
I'll breathe again, for that, I'm sure.
A tonic for this, a mantra for that,
A séance for stress, a capsule for cats.

With potions of plenty and herbs in a can,
I'm even allergic to the medicine man!

IN SEARCH OF THE COLOR YELLOW

Today I went on a walk
in search of the color yellow

Blind to myself
and my emotions
I was not wearing
yellow today

I waved to the man
in a faded yellow van
and noticed the sullen
look on his face

I continued my search
for yellow

I walked past the man
in the suit of black
but did not say, "hi"
and never looked back

I, too, was invisible to him
he was blind to all colors
except his colors within

I sat upon a yellow curb
and cried for choices led by
greed or pride

Barefoot I strolled
through colorless grass
to the edge of town
I so often passed

On a clothesline
yellow satin sheets danced
in enlightened thought
I gazed, entranced

I looked to the sky
I once believed to be blue
and saw plunging streaks
of golden hues

Today I went on a walk
and found the color yellow

VOLUME 2

BALLAD OF THE WOLVES

In a forest bathed in crimson glow
The grass was scarce with speckled snow
A cold wind slowly howled and creaked
Through dismal wood devoid of sleep

Ignited by shafts of glowing light
'Twas woods by day and dream by night
A figure emerged, a silhouette
Entangled in vines of her regret

Perhaps entrapped by lovers past
An anger boiled inside her chest
She sliced the vines with jagged knife
Then listened for carnal signs of life

Eerie quiet soon was shattered
A crunching sound, a drumming patter
With flickers of white-tinged eyes
A pack of phantom wolves arrived

She ran to release the rage inside
She ran with the wolves to feel alive
As she began to breathe anew
The dream dispersed, as all dreams do

ARGUMENT WITH A SHADOW

I hear you breathing,
I know it's not the wind

A shadow lurks
He won't forget
A pulsing heart,
A silhouette

I lock the doors
I shut the blinds
I shift my thoughts
To lighter times

I remember him
From years ago
I loved him once
But let him go

Knock, knock, knock
Upon my door
A hungry shadow
Begs for more

Turn off the lights!
In vain, I hide
The phantom slides
His way inside

"Remember me?"
He whispers slow
"It's past the time
For you to go!"

Forget, forget
The heartless taunt
Find another
Soul to haunt

I hear you breathing,
I know it's not the wind

WINTER ORCHARD

A breath sweeps over rolling hills
In the bitter air, an icy chill
Perhaps just a collective sigh
As barren arms plead to a rusted sky

Embedded deeply in the dirt below
My trunk entwined with whirling snow
Branches iced from winter freeze
Amongst rows and rows of vacant trees

Though pale and stark most every day
There's a place my daydreams sway
A skeletal angel, I wait and wait
As if in line for heaven's gate

Days and days go slowly by
I reach towards the ocher sky
As sun releases streaks of calm
A golden apple grows in my palm

SHADOWS, STONES, SOULS, BONES

Sun shines upon the stone,
A shadow hovers over her bones
He drifts 'til dusk; he drifts 'til dawn
He cannot fathom she is gone

Whirling in the whining wind
Tumbleweed rolls, and then rescinds
Rays of light dwindle and die
A silhouette refutes goodbye

Shadows, stones, souls, bones
For his regrets, can he atone?
There was a time she took his stone,
A diamond wrapped in band of gold

Neighbors heard the fatal shot
That drove her to her resting plot
A silhouette with sinister soul
Craved for her complete control

Somewhere in the earth below
Lays a soulless grave; she decided to go
Whispers, rain, wind, pain
Her breath was lost, but not in vain

She trailed the sun and followed its rays
To a warm embrace of endless days
Where love is dusk; love is dawn
He cannot find her here, she's gone

HAIKU FOR THE DEPARTED

Laughing train whistles
Racketing blue thunder rolls
Turn back, wait for me

DOVES AND CROWS

Once upon an endless night
Her home engulfed with amber light
Lost in swirling smoke and flames
Alone, a lifeless body lay

A spirit watched from far afield
Her heart was broke, her senses reeled
Home to ashes, dreams to dust
She lost her life in a single puff

What happened next was kind of weird
A swirl of peculiar shapes appeared
Out of the smoke, a darkness rose
A cycling murder of screaming crows!

A vengeance filled her vacant veins
Her arms transformed to feathered wings
Her eyes reformed to beady black
She rebirthed as a bird of raged attack

"Revenge, revenge!" the crows all chanted
"Stalk the souls," they squawked and ranted
Vengeance was the song they sung
"It wasn't your time, you died too young!"

Then a flash of white soared from above
Amongst the flock flew a single dove
She paused to reflect upon her wrongs
Though hate was fierce, hope was strong

Some say young souls come back in black
Revived as birds of avenged attack
The woman's wings faded to white
She trailed the dove to the end of night

THE TRANSIENT POET

The road, the wide-open road,
My chosen home.
The stretching, endless ribbon of black
The path in which I roam.

If I am lost, do not worry
I have not ventured far.
I am seeking all that matters
Under the guide of falling stars.

Life is but a passing home
A delay before the dark.
We are running out of breath
On this journey, we embark.

The road is not all revelation,
It is hunger, desire, and dust.
I ponder, did we build the roads
Or did the roads build us?

All roads lead to home
When home is on the street.
'Tis a peaceful place to wander
I'll return, again we'll meet.

God gave me a compass
When I lost my way.
She asked me to find my purpose
So, I wrote this poem today.

When twilight comes upon you,
Remember my closing plea.
Savor the sunset, it may be
The last you'll ever see.

THE CLOCKSMITH

Uncle Chester made a thousand clocks
He hammered, nailed, cut wood in blocks
He hung a clock on the ceiling and wall
By the fireplace, the stove, in the front hall

Oh, what a curious man was he
The maker of minutes was hero to me
The townsfolk lined up, begging for time
They bartered and pushed their place in line

The doctor, the mayor, the farmer, the teacher
The writer, the baker, the fighter, the preacher
They knocked and knocked and knocked once more
But Uncle Chester never opened his door

I guess he passed at half past one
A complete surprise to everyone
So, the moral of this quirky rhyme
Uncle Chester could not make more time

SUFFERING SILENTLY

Abandoned tunnel for a winter home
Burdened by the grim, daunting smile
Of Grief and Loss that plagues us all
Though he has nothing, he has words
And rhyme to comfort him. He lies alone
Under a ripped patchwork blanket
Reading the rhythmic phrases
Of yesterday's pompous and love-drunk poets
Who wrote of daydreams, hopes, trials, and betrayal.
He is freezing, fidgety, and full of despair.
A business woman walks briskly to her nine-to-five life.
He cannot fathom her hurry nor her
Mechanical method in which she survives.
He sees the world through timeless eyes,
He watches snowflakes crystallize,
Business shoes trample on nature's path
And crash the beauty that lies before him.

SMOKE AND STARS

A night shadow lengthens through a gaping tunnel.
A figure illuminates, smoking meditatively as he
Stares at nothing and thinks about everything.
A great strangeness consumes him. A slow, intuitive
Process of renewing, forgetting, fondling
His Marlboro as he exhales sweltering subtleties
Of solitude. He exits the tunnel in a moment of
Brevity and belonging, and gazes at Orion the Hunter,
The hero Perseus, and the demon star Algol.
Twilight twinkles. He takes another drag
Of downward thoughts, as his mood plummets
Like a burned-out star. He ambles the iron tracks.
A slow howl of a train screams in his abyss.

RIVERSIDE CARNIVAL

Seagulls, seagulls soaring near
It was a day of hope,
It was a night of fear

Roller coaster, roller coaster
Riverside town
What goes up
Will come crashing down

Her emotions were
A whirling mess,
She craved a cure
For worthlessness

Ferris wheel, ferris wheel
A bridge to the sky
Whirling, twirling
She soared so high

She climbed inside
A photo booth
To capture the essence
Of fleeting youth

Twirling, twirling
Tilter whirl
She was alone, she was alone
Just an empty girl

Zoltar, Zoltar
Want a fortune? Pull the lever!
You will never have luck
If you stay in this endeavor

Seagulls, seagulls soaring near
It was a day of hope,
It was a night of fear

THE GHOST OF FOUNTAIN CITY

Just a mile from the lock and dam,
On the Great River Road, a marshy land
Wedged between a river and bluff,
Stand buildings of teal, yellow, and rust

The townsfolk say that ghosts live here
In the old saloon, they drink their beer
And just as folks forget their fear,
Their glasses up and disappear

The boneyard's a place they all know
Under the moon, the stones aglow
The one dated eighteen twenty-nine,
That grave, I do confess, is mine

At midnight when the town bell tolls,
I slither out and take a stroll
Though it's getting very late,
I crawl beneath the iron gate

Please don't fear, and oh don't pity
I too am a ghost of Fountain City
I once wore a suit and a mayor's hat
Was honored by all, but that was that

This town was rich in farming land
Settlers came with hired hand
The train brought coal, left with grain
People changed, yet it's all the same

Wedged between a river and bluff
Stand buildings of teal, yellow, and rust
Population eight hundred and fifty-nine
Plus a thousand souls, and one is mine

FISHERMAN ON KUAMOO ROAD

On the island of Kauai
At close of graveled road
They parked their dusty rental car
Where glist'ning waters flowed

Eucalyptus lined the bank
Rays sprayed 'pon hats of straw
The tourists cast a drunken stare
A merge of wonder and awe

Standing 'pon graffitied bridge
Leathered skin and eyes of stone
A fishpole firmly in his hands
'Twas a man who trawled alone

He assured the sun brought creek
But storm, a surging river
As droplets fell upon their cheeks
The two began to quiver

A pattering of hands on drums
Distant chanting, spirit wind
They thanked him, then strolled away
A breath behind the bend

"Turn back, let's take his photograph"
As the rising river flowed
They returned to just a vacant bridge
At the end of Kuamoo Road

MIDNIGHT ON PEARL STREET

An eerie moon on Pearl Street
Lit her crimson shawl
On a midnight stroll, floated the soul
Of the late Ms. Frankie LeSalle

She held a lace umbrella
Covering coils of auburn hair
Rain misted on the fabric
As she cast a lonely stare

She sauntered into the tavern
On the corner of Fourth and Cass
Then sat upon the barstool
And caressed an empty glass

Candles gently flickered
Smells of cigars and beer
On a late-night bet sat the silhouette
Of the lumberman, James Granier

Meanwhile, on Pearl Street
A hunt of his own embarked
On a twilight course, he galloped on horse
'Twas the night watch, Officer Parks

His shadow in a ragged hat
With a lantern of kerosene
Prowled the city in search
Of the sinuous underworld queen

Daybreak on Pearl Street
A horizon of ember hues
Fog lifted like rising spirits
As the underworld bade adieu

RAIN PUDDLES ON WEAVER LAKE DRIVE

It was a summer morning, or so I remember.
I was five years old, wearing yellow rain boots.
My mood was amber like the faint morning rays
That pierced through my living room window
Where I pensively gazed.

Rain droplets tapped on the glass, like playful spirits
Knocking and whispering, "Come outside."
As I peered through the window, I wondered
If the end of the world was the cul-de-sac of Weaver Lake Drive.

I slammed the screen door and splashed across the street
To echoes of drizzling rain descending into a sewer.
As the droplets turned to a downpour, the rain pooled
On the pavement. Carelessly, I stomped in a puddle,
Listening as the gushing rain echoed towards me.

I didn't know at the time, but at that moment
I found the sensation I would later search for, in vain.
The comfort of innocence, forgiveness of rain, and harmony
That comes from humble moments like splashing in rain puddles.

I didn't know beyond Weaver Lake Drive, a windy gravel road
Would lead to a church. One day, I would carry yellow roses
Down an aisle leading to dropped pedals of loss and despair.

Years later, I walked the midnight streets alone,
Wearing a pale summer dress and high heels. My mood was
Blood red like an angry sun slinking behind the clouds at dusk.

As I sauntered the streets, a cold rain fell upon my shoulders.
Droplets turned to a downpour. Rain pooled on the pavement.
Under a golden street light, I paused at a puddle and gazed at my
Reflection: just a child wearing rain boots with a grin on her face.

Carelessly, I stomped in the puddle. Listening, as the gushing rain
Echoed towards me.

I KNEW AN OLD COWBOY
-A Tribute

I knew an old cowboy, who didn't wear boots
He wore a crooked smile and a business suit

He never rode horseback, never roped bull
He had a wild soul; his life was full

He never stood still, no, he wasn't that man
He drove mile after mile in his Chevy van

How was he a cowboy? This question is fair
He breathed for thrills and abandoned all care

He did not sleep by a desolate fire
The west wind whistling upon his pyre

He lassoed sunsets of amber rays
Corralled the lonely with a gentle embrace

He wasn't quick with a rifle or knife
He had bullets of smiles and a happy life

They say, "Only the good die young."
After fifty-nine years, his hat was hung

My father was a cowboy, a legend of mine
A man I wish to talk to, a thousand times

Cowboys leave trails of lessons learned
He left me his kindness and all that he yearned

I knew an old cowboy.

VIETNAM SKY

Many years ago, in 'Nam
Above the South China Sea
Three pilots in formation flew
Mac, Joey, and me

The Vietnam sky was painted
Hues of umber and gray
Scent of smoke and sea water
Infused the summer day

Three Navy Skyhawks rose
We climbed through rival haze
Then dove a daring plunge
Through a trail of heaven's rays

An enemy plane perched and preyed
Near the battlefield by the sea
Missiles aimed at rising aircraft
Flown by Mac, Joey, and me

My path diverged to higher sky
I hid in the clouds from harm
Then the tender grace of angels
Embraced my plane into their arms

My brothers bravely bolted
From the airborne attack
Smoke and metal filled the cockpits
Igniting the planes of Joey and Mac

The salty seawater swallowed
Two soldiers that summer day
Angels lowered me to the shore
Where I kneeled to weep and pray

Spirits embalmed the aircrafts
Submerged in the brine of death
Pulse by pulse, Joey and Mac
Exhaled their closing breaths

Many nights I softly dream
I return to the South China Sea
Greeted by two phantom planes
And we forever fly as three

GHOST TRAIN

The old red engine
Is covered in rust
The poet ascends
To her boxcar of dust

Lovers come
Lovers go
A train embarks
On a rail of snow

Chuga, chuga
Choo, choo, choo
The businessman
Polishes his shoe

One by one,
Passengers erase
They disappear
Without a trace

Devoid of emotion,
The train is a ghost
The poet searches
For her invisible host

"Conductor, conductor
Don't leave me alone
On this train of illusion,
I want to go home!"

Alone in the boxcar
The woman remains
The sky fades to night
She is haunted with shame

Caboose, caboose
In rhythmic bounce
The end is near
Renounce, renounce

The train screeches
To a poetic halt
She leaves alone
It is all her fault

Engine, wheels
Steam and brakes
The woman in sorrow
And solitude...escapes!

She flees the station
High heels in hand
She runs and runs
As fast as she can

But a familiar bell
Stops her in her tracks
She turns to see a man
In a conductor's hat

She returns to the train
And they embrace
In the fog, he places
A kiss on her face

"Conductor, conductor,
Where have you been?
The train turned to dust
I was alone again!"

"Lantern, boxcar,
Rail and junction
I am your conductor,
My sole function

Just when you thought
You were riding alone
I grabbed the wheel
And drove you home

Through winter's wrath
And all your pain
Someone has
To drive your train!"

The woman in yellow
Disappeared in the dust
Left the conductor alone
Beside his engine of rust

A story is never
Quite what it seems,
A steamy ride
Much like a dream

Lovers come
Lovers go
A train embarks
On a rail of snow

Acknowledgements

Thank you first and foremost to my family for your patience, love, and support. Thank you, Saveah, for your contributions to "Doves and Crows," "Ballad of the Wolves," and "The Woman on top of the Hill." Gavin, thank you for your unwavering kindness and for venturing with me to write, "The Ghost of Fountain City." Thank you to my parents who have encouraged me to find my passions.

To Shannon and Orange Hat Publishing, thank you for trusting in my poetry. I appreciate your encouragement to publish *Waiting for Red* and *In Search of the Color Yellow* as a duology. To my editor, Lauren, thank you for your steady guidance, detailed eye, and expertise. I am fortunate to collaborate with a team of professionals.

La Crosse Area Writer's Group, thank you for your friendships and encouragement. We have devoted countless hours to our passion of writing, critiquing, and finding "just the right word." Special appreciation to the members who provided a review of the manual. Your suggestions were invaluable.

Thank you, Anthony, for your professional photograph that perfectly matched the vision of *In Search of the Color Yellow* as an entrance into the dark unknown.

Wagonbridge Publishing, thank you for including "Where Does the Tumbleweed Roll" and "Vietnam Sky" in the anthology *Lost and Found.*

Thank you to the passengers on my "Ghost Train," people who have come and gone but left shadows, imprints, memories. Perhaps a passing glance, a friendship shared, a recollection of a moment in time that stuck with me.

I always thought if I searched hard enough, I would find the color "yellow" in my future. As if I walked through the dark tunnel, I would see that glimmer of light and inspiration I was missing. But the more I think about it, all I need to find "yellow" is to reflect and remember. A barefoot walk through a field of goldenrod. Yesterday's butterflies. An aged, yellow photograph of my father. I have always been surrounded by yellow, but just did not notice it was there.

K.L. Schoberg lives and writes in Southwest Wisconsin with her two children. She is a University of Wisconsin-La Crosse graduate who studied Psychology and Writing. A devoted social worker, she is committed to her community.

An advocate for poetry, Kelly organizes a monthly critique group with the La Crosse Area Writer's Group. When she is not writing, she enjoys reciting her works at open microphone events. Influences of her poetry include La Crosse Area Writer's Group, Chippewa Valley Writer's Guild, Winona Fine Arts Commission, and Wisconsin Fellowship of Poets.

In Search of the Color Yellow and *Waiting for Red* are her first published books.

klschoberg.com
Find her on Facebook: K.L. Schoberg, Author

www.ingramcontent.com/pod-product-compliance
Lightning Source LLC
Chambersburg PA
CBHW070801050426
42452CB00012B/2437